Highlands

.... **National borders**

0   800 km

CAMBODIA

VIETNAM

SOUTH
CHINA
SEA

THE PHILIPPINES

MALAYSIA

PACIFIC
OCEAN

• Medan

Sumatra

• Singapore

BORNEO

Kalimantan

Maluku

Irian Jaya

• Bangka

Celebes

Ceram

NEW
GUINEA

N

W E

S

I N D O N E S I A

• Jakarta

Java

Madura

Bali Sumbawa Flores

Lombok

Sumba

Timor

I N D I A N   O C E A N

AUSTRALIA

▷ The
islands of
Indonesia.

Special features

▽ The active
volcano Merapi is
surrounded by
ricefields, farms
and villages.

Some of Indonesia's islands have been formed from
volcanoes. Some of the volcanoes are old and worn
down. Others are new and still dangerous, throwing out
hot rocks, ash and gas when they erupt. But eruptions
bring up fresh minerals from deep in the Earth that
make the land very good for farming.
The islands of Java and Bali have
always had high populations, because
of the fertile soil and regular rainfall.

If you climb the mountains of
Kalimantan or Irian Jaya, you'll fight
through thick rainforest until it's too
high even for trees to grow. By contrast,
the islands of the south-east seem bare,
with grassy plains that are dry for
much of the year.

The sea is an important part of
Indonesia, too. Beautiful coral reefs
fringe many of the islands. In fact
Indonesia covers more water than land.

3

The people

Hundreds of thousands of years ago, when northern Europe was still covered by ice, there were already people living on Java using fire and tools. Today's Indonesians have ancestors from as far away as Melanesia, southern China and Vietnam. Java and Sumatra first **developed** under Malay and Indian influences.

Religion and culture

Indian culture brought writing, the potter's wheel, and textile dyeing. It also brought new religions, **Hinduism** and **Buddhism**. Indonesian puppet and dance plays still tell stories from the Hindu legends.

Buddhism and Hinduism appealed to the ruling classes. But when the new faith of **Islam** reached ordinary people, with the important idea that we are all equal in the eyes of God, it was very popular. Today there are more **Muslims** living in Indonesia than in any other single country.

People of all these different religions still live by **adat**, the traditional Indonesian laws of social behaviour.

Trade and the Europeans

Muslim traders were attracted by the precious woods and spices that grow in Indonesia. And when pepper, cloves, cinnamon and nutmeg were sent to Europe, merchants there soon set sail to find the famous 'Spice Islands' for themselves.

△ **This Balinese dancer is telling a story from Hindu mythology.**

Traders from all over Europe fought for control of the islands, but in 1602 the Dutch East India Company put themselves in charge and made the 'East Indies' a colony. By the nineteenth century, people were forced to grow crops like coffee and rubber for the Dutch, instead of food to eat. They often went hungry. After the second World War and their own bitter fight, the people finally won Independence and formed the new country of Indonesia. With 250 languages in the archipelago, they needed to pick one in common and **Bahasa Indonesia** became the official language.

A new country

The first government made many plans to help the people. But in 1965 there was a violent change of power, when many people were killed. Since then, President Suharto has been ruler, and his government is very tightly controlled.

When the Dutch and Portuguese finally left the nearby colonies of West Papua and East Timor, the Indonesian government took them over (and re-named West Papua 'Irian Jaya'). But for many of the people in these territories, Indonesia is like another foreign country.

▽ Dutch colonialists built this as a city hall in Jakarta. It is now a museum.

Where do people live?

Altogether, 185 million people live in Indonesia, but they're not evenly spread. Although the island of Java has only seven per cent of the land area, sixty per cent of the people live there. Imagine over 100 million people living on an island just over half the size of Britain! Such a dense population puts great pressure on the environment.

Transmigration

The government has tried moving people from Java to other islands where fewer people live. But this causes tension because local people feel their way of life is being threatened. And the **migrants** themselves can't always live as they would have back in Java. Their way of farming is often not suitable for the thinner soil on other islands.

City life and country life

Millions of people are still moving to the island of Java every year. Almost all of Indonesia's new industry is based here and the capital city, Jakarta, is the centre of government and business power.

▽ The capital city of Jakarta with its skyscrapers and kampung settlements.

△ This traditional house in Rantepao on Celebes has a roof shaped like buffalo horns. There are two long sleeping rooms upstairs and one big room downstairs.

Life in the city is very hard for ordinary people. But many are attracted by the idea that there may be a better life for them here than they had in their home village, where perhaps they had no land to farm and no hope of a job. Some come to work in the factories or as street traders and send money home, planning to return some day. Many will end up staying for the rest of their lives.

Places to live

In the city, new migrants usually move into a crowded **kampung** settlement. But there are modern flats too, and expensive, concrete Western-style houses.

The country is changing quickly, but throughout the islands many people still live in traditional houses that suit their different ways of life.

In northern Sumatra, large houses built on wooden pillars are decorated with carvings and buffalo horns. In the south of the island, forest dwellers live in houses built in the trees.

Farther east, in the dry grassy landscape of Sumba, traditional houses are like giant straw hats. On Bali, compounds are kept private with high walls. But in the forests of Irian Jaya and Kalimantan, whole clans live together in shared 'long houses'.

Agriculture

Three out of five Indonesian people work on the land. Many are **subsistence farmers**, growing only enough to feed their families. But some work to grow **cash crops** to sell in the cities and to **export**.

Most farmers are smallholders. On crowded islands like Java and Bali, the average farm is only half a hectare. But it's warm all year round, with plenty of rain and rich, black volcanic soil. Farmers here can grow two or three crops each year on the same field.

Rice and other crops

Rice is Indonesia's most important crop. Villagers' rice fields are usually watered in turn and they often share the buffalo or tractor used for ploughing. New rice seeds, which produce more grain, are being sold to farmers. But these need costly chemical fertilizers and pesticides, which can be harmful to the environment.

▽ **Buffaloes help churn up the flooded soil before rice seedlings are planted.**

Away from Java and Bali, many of the other islands aren't so fertile, and crops like corn, cassava, sweet potatoes and the sago palm are more important. In rainforest areas some people live by hunting wild animals and collecting food plants. On islands like Flores, Sumba and Timor, people clear patches of land to grow crops for one or two seasons, then move on. Oxfam is working with dryland farmers in these places to find ways of growing crops in settled farms without spoiling the land.

Produce and land

After oil, cash crops are Indonesia's most important export. When Indonesia was a Dutch **colony**, land was taken to grow rubber, coffee, tea, cocoa and sugar for people in Europe. After independence, some of this land was given back to the local people. But a lot is still being used by cash crop businesses while smaller farmers are running out of land.

Land is also used up by companies for property development, mining, power plants or even tourist resorts. Each time farmers pass land on to their children there is less to share out between them. Land shortage is one reason people **migrate** to the cities to find work.

△ A farmer in Java cuts her second rice crop this year before planting sweet potatoes.

Industry

Indonesia has always traded its **natural resources**. At first spices were most important, then crops like rubber and coffee. Later it started to **export** timber, coal and oil. Indonesia is the biggest producer of natural gas in the world.

Now the government is encouraging **manufacturing** industries that make raw materials more valuable by turning them into finished goods like tee-shirts or toys. Most of these industries are on Java. About seven per cent of the whole population work in factories, but the number is growing.

These sport shoes will be exported to the United States and Europe. It would take a worker here two or three months to earn enough money to buy a pair.

Low wages

Transnational companies can move their work around the world. They set up business wherever raw materials are cheapest and taxes are lowest, or where people are paid the least. This means that the companies can keep more money as profit when they sell their goods.

Wages in Indonesia are kept extremely low to attract the transnational companies and their jobs. Many workers are paid barely enough money to live on. This is because government fears that if wages were higher, these big companies would go somewhere cheaper.

Traditional industries

Indonesian people have always made and decorated things. They do this not only for profit, but also for pleasure, as seen in the carved posts of Sumatran houses and the ornate **wayang** costumes.

Their traditional carvings and textiles are famous around the world. But these days most customers are tourists, and they can't always tell the difference between a hand-made object and a factory copy.

The tourist trade

Most tourists come to enjoy Indonesia's beautiful scenery and hot weather. Bali is very popular. Many people come here to sunbathe, visit the temples, climb volcanoes and scuba-dive on the coral reefs.

▽ In the early morning tourists on Bali are taken on outrigger boats to search for dolphins.

Tourism is an important source of **foreign exchange** for the country, but it can damage the environment. Local people sometimes even have to leave their villages to make way for tourist resorts.

Challenges

Indonesia's natural resources were the reason the islands were colonised. Now they are being sold to raise money for internal development, and to pay back loans from other countries.

Indonesia's environment challenge

Indonesia's challenge is to balance these demands against the real needs of the people now and in the future. For example, the government can raise money by selling fishing permits to foreign factory ships, but if too many fish are caught they might die out altogether.

Mining has harmful effects, too. The land is damaged, rivers polluted and local people forced away. Most seriously, the forests being cut and sold as timber will probably never recover. Once the land is bare of trees, **monsoon** rains can cause floods and landslides. And the forests are homes for people as well as wildlife.

Biodiversity

The animals and plants that have adapted to life in Indonesia are very varied. So we say that Indonesia has a high biodiversity.

▽ Today there are only about 100 Javan rhinoceros.

To the west, animals and plants are more like those found in Asia. There are tigers, leopards and the nearly-extinct Javan rhinoceros. Kalimantan has 21 types of monkeys and apes. Farther east there are animals with pouches, like those in Australia. Altogether Indonesia has more plant species than does the whole of Africa or America. This diversity is put at risk when mining and logging companies are invited onto the land.

△ Local people won't be able to feed their families if the factory ships take too many fish.

Problems for the people

Local people find it hard to live in their traditional ways and to be **self-sufficient** in areas where the natural resources are being exploited. For example, Irian Jaya now has huge copper and gold mines. A quarter of Indonesia's export earnings come from the coal, oil and gas extracted from Kalimantan. These places are being changed forever as forests are cut, new roads built and **transmigrants** move in bringing new and different lifestyles.

National parks and tourism

Nature and marine reserves and national parks have been set up, where logging, fishing and mining are not supposed to be allowed. But sometimes this means local people are forbidden to enter or use the forests or seas that their families have used for centuries, while mining or fishing companies are still allowed in.

Jatiwakas

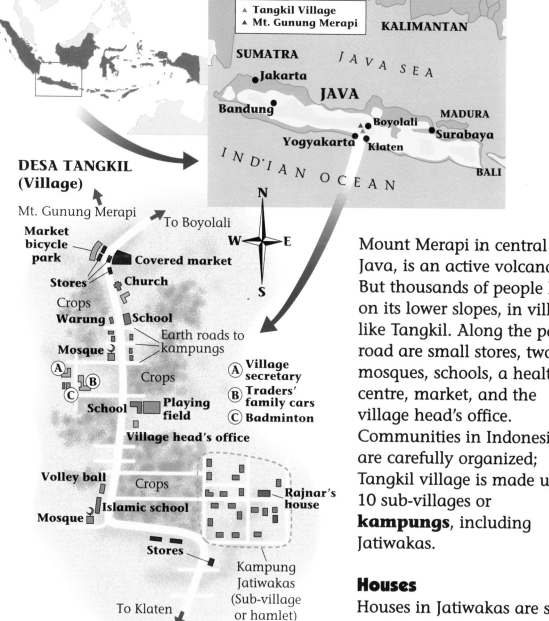

Map legend:
▲ Tangkil Village
▲ Mt. Gunung Merapi

KALIMANTAN

SUMATRA

J A V A   S E A

Jakarta

JAVA

Bandung

MADURA

Boyolali

Surabaya

Yogyakarta   Klaten

I N D I A N   O C E A N

BALI

DESA TANGKIL (Village)

Mt. Gunung Merapi

To Boyolali

N

W   E

S

Market bicycle park

Covered market

Stores   Church

Crops

Warung   School

Earth roads to kampungs

Mosque

Ⓐ

Ⓒ   Ⓑ

Crops

School   Playing field

Ⓐ Village secretary
Ⓑ Traders' family cars
Ⓒ Badminton

Village head's office

Volley ball   Crops

Islamic school   Rajnar's house

Mosque

Stores

Kampung Jatiwakas (Sub-village or hamlet)

To Klaten

△ Java and the village of Tangkil showing the Jatiwakas kampung.

Mount Merapi in central Java, is an active volcano. But thousands of people live on its lower slopes, in villages like Tangkil. Along the paved road are small stores, two mosques, schools, a health centre, market, and the village head's office. Communities in Indonesia are carefully organized; Tangkil village is made up of 10 sub-villages or **kampungs**, including Jatiwakas.

Houses

Houses in Jatiwakas are still made in the traditional style, woven bamboo on a wooden frame. Most families have clay tiles on their roofs and concrete rainwater tanks.

There are separate rooms for cooking, and for sleeping and socializing, with a bamboo platform covered in mats making a big bed in one corner. But there are no windows; it's fairly dark inside even in the daytime.

△ A path through the village.

Farming in Jatiwakas

Families here grow rice, cassava, corn and chillies in the ground, and tree crops like jackfruit and cloves. They keep chickens and goats, and a new government scheme is encouraging them to keep cows as well.

Tangkil is 900 metres above sea level and although the topsoil is fertile, just below is the hard rock of the volcano. The ground is too hard to hold water, and wells are impossible to dig. The nearest river is seven kilometres away, so people depend on rain for their water supply.

Between November and March, rain falls heavily onto the fields and from the steep, tiled roofs into the water tanks. But from April to October, it hardly ever rains and the tanks have to be used for farming as well as the household. Some people buy water from a visiting tanker to top-up their rainwater tanks, but it's still hard to keep the fields watered in the dry season.

Village life

△ Clothes being washed at the nearest river, seven kilometres from Jatiwakas.

Both men and women work hard in Jatiwakas, but the women have a double workload as they work around the house as well as the farm. This means feeding the animals, washing clothes and gathering fuel as well as cooking and cleaning.

Most of the children go to school for at least a few years. But they are expected to sweep the earth floors and the yard before breakfast, and help feed the animals in the afternoon.

Organizations

Tangkil has a village head and secretary appointed by the government. They know everything that goes on in the different **kampungs**, and recently organized electricity for Tangkil village. But the different kampungs also have their own organizations.

Most married men and women belong to a savings club. Each week every member contributes an equal amount of money, and they take turns to receive the whole amount. It might be used for house improvements or to buy seeds, to buy clothes for the family, or to buy a new goat.

The teenagers have their own groups, too, and usually meet at the mosque to study, chat and play volleyball. They recently clubbed together to buy a tape recorder and loudspeaker for the mosque – and for parties.

Village needs

People hope that the new electricity supply will soon reach more houses in the village, although not everyone wants television. 'There are some useful educational programmes. But so many of the American films are violent or immodest,' says the teacher.

What people in Jatiwakas and Tangkil really want is a reliable water system. The village can't afford it themselves. 'If we had a golf course for tourists, the water supply would soon be arranged!' said one man.

▽ People who live near volcanoes always fear eruptions. This village near Tangkil was recently destroyed. Because of the constant risk, villages on the side of Mount Merapi practise evacuation and first aid.

School

Education is important to Javanese families. Most of the children in Jatiwakas go to elementary school despite the cost of uniforms and books.

Rajnar is eleven and has almost finished at Tangkil II elementary school. He leaves the house at 7 a.m. and usually he's at school until lunchtime – even on Saturdays.

What do they study?

There's a lot to study: first, the national language, **Bahasa Indonesia**, as well as his local language of Javanese. Then there's maths, science and social studies like history, geography and 'PANCASILA,' the political beliefs of the state. Not forgetting religious studies, domestic science, art and crafts, and of course, sports.

'Today we had Bahasa Indonesia and maths. I want to stay on at school and study maths – its my favourite. Maths and football.'

Plans and dreams

Older children have to travel by bus or bicycle to get to the secondary schools. Winarni is Rajnar's neighbour in Jatiwakas and she is in grade three of senior high school in Klaten.

'I come home to my family on Friday afternoons but every Sunday I get the bus back to Klaten and my boarding house. Luckily I'm in the top stream so I can take science. It's hard for me to see the future, but I would love to go to the university in Yogyakarta to train as a scientist. And in the city you have so much more information – radio, TV, newspapers; I want to improve my understanding of the world.'

△ Here is Rajnar in his school uniform.

▷ Some older children travel a long way to attend school each day.

Indonesia has some very good universities, but it's hard for someone from an ordinary family to afford the fees. Most students leaving high school head for the cities to look for work in the factories there. Rajnar's elder brother works in a clothes factory in Jakarta, hundreds of kilometres away. He comes home every few months to see his wife and their new baby but will probably never move back permanently.

Some children are happy to see their future in the village. 'I want to be a farmer like my father, and he's teaching me how to be a carpenter, too,' says Rajnar's cousin, Arifin.

△ Rajnar sitting at his school desk.

Spare time

After school Rajnar is free to play before settling down to his homework. 'When it's raining I go to the house that has television. But most days I'll go and cut grass for the cow. When it gets big enough we'll sell it and get another small one. My dad will give me some of the money. I'll spend some on sweets but mostly it's for my school graduation.'

Arifin, Rajnar's cousin, helps a lot more at home. Rajnar's uncle died a few years ago, so his aunt has a farm to look after as well as her small shop. But relatives usually stay close in Indonesia, and Arifin's family is only one house away so there is always advice and help.

Games

Younger children make model **kampungs** in the mud or play with whistles made from banana leaves and sticks. They play Indonesian 'tag' or 'it' as well.

▽ These children are playing a jumping game called sprinter.

'If you're "it" and you catch someone else, you have to carry them on your back for a while. It's silly, but we laugh a lot,' says Rajnar.

Badminton is very popular. Susi Susanti, the women's world champion for many years, is from Indonesia.

Culture

The adults have less time to relax, but after a good harvest the kampung might club together to hire a travelling **wayang** theatre show. And Tangkil has its own gamelan orchestra, to play for the wayang performance. It will also come to your house for special occasions.

A Javanese gamelan orchestra makes a very special sort of music. There are xylophones, drums and gongs made of metal, wood and skin, some stringed instruments and perhaps a bamboo flute. Each member of the orchestra has many instruments to play, and although the music is very complicated it is not often written down.

△ The equipment might be a bit old, but badminton is played seriously in Tangkil.

In the cities, there is more to do, if you have the money. Many men will simply gather at a street stall to drink coffee, play chess and talk – perhaps about their families back in the village.

A day in Jatiwakas

On the slopes of the mountain, the nights are cooler than in the lowlands and it's easier to sleep. But the chickens will still wake everyone in the village by four or five o'clock in the misty morning. And everywhere the women are up early, cooking for their families.

▷ Rajnar's father and sister coming back from the fields.

The working day

Before going to work in the fields, Rajnar's father, Pak Kito, has rice, tofu – curd made from soybeans – and tea for his breakfast. People in central Java love sweet things, and tea is usually made without milk but with plenty of sugar. Rajnar's mother, Ibu Rajiman, might go with Pak Kito to work in the fields. Otherwise, she has more cleaning and cooking to do before her husband and son return.

Rajnar's sister, Warini, doesn't go to school any more. This morning she gathers firewood for cooking, and cuts jackfruit from the trees to take to tomorrow's market. She makes a fire with coconut husks to cook rice crackers. There are hundreds of different kinds; some are thin and spicy, some flavoured with shrimps or peanuts. Today Warini is using last night's leftover rice to make thick, crunchy, sweet ones.

▽ Village boys cut grass for their cow.

In the afternoon Rajnar gathers leaves and grass for the cow, and his mother collects the dung to use as a natural fertilizer for their fields.

Evening

It gets dark quickly at around 6 p.m., and the first rains of the new season bring out flying termites in their millions. Houses with electric light are soon filled with their beating wings. Rajnar and his friends take a kerosene lamp outside to attract the termites and collect them in a bowl of water. They're delicious fried to eat right away, or they can make a little money selling them in the market tomorrow. It's fun, and a distraction from the neighbour's TV!

The family settle down to sleep one by one, but by 9 or 10 p.m. even Ibu Rajiman has finished her chores and they're all snuggled up on the bamboo platforms.

Tonight there's a celebration in Jatiwakas. A new baby has reached 40 days old, and his family have hired the gamelan for a party. The rest of the village drift off to sleep lulled by its dreamlike, gonging sound.

Travel around Jatiwakas

Tangkil village has four motor vehicles – but they all belong to the trader's family, higher up the mountain. People in Jatiwakas depend on bicycles, motorbikes and the bus service for transport.

Roads

Because Tangkil is on the road between Boyolali and Klaten, regular buses pass through the village every day. Some of the children commute to school on the bus, others ride bicycles. Most people will walk around Tangkil itself, but the main road is steep because it is on the side of the mountain. So if you have the fare, the bus is well worth it – especially on the way up to the top of the village where the market is held.

▽ It's a long walk uphill to the market. You can see Mount Merapi volcano in the background.

The market

At the market itself, people have come from as far as the district capital, Yogyakarta, nearly 50 kilometres away. Local people come to sell vegetables and tree crops from their land – rice, corn, bananas, coconuts and jackfruit, and special crops like cloves and tree beans.

Ibu Rajiman feeds her family mostly from the farm, but once she's sold her corn and jackfruit, she will buy extras like tea and sugar, cooking oil, some kerosene for the lamps and a new shirt for Rajnar.

The road to Klaten descends to flatter, wetter land where **irrigated** rice fields – paddies – are being planted. The rainy season isn't so important here. There is water all year around, so more people live here. The land is easier to farm, and some of it is owned by the government, or by big companies, growing large areas of **cash crops** like sugar and tobacco.

△ A local woman sells jackfruit to a visitor from Yogyakarta.

Buses and trucks carrying people, goods and crops race along the road past oxcarts, bicycles and pedestrians. Goods sell in Klaten for a small profit; but the crops in the trucks going to Yogyakarta and Jakarta will fetch much higher prices for the owners.

Journeys around Indonesia

The map at the beginning of this book will remind you just how big Indonesia is. For people who can afford the fares, there is a good network of airports and airlines, and some people do have private cars. For most, journeys around the country take longer.

△ A three-wheeler car in Jakarta.

In the towns, bicycles adapted to carry passengers are convenient for short journeys. They've been banned inside the capital city, Jakarta, where instead small three-wheeled motor vehicles add to the pollution.

Outside the city, a range of bigger and bigger buses cover longer and longer distances. On Sumatra and Java it's still possible to take a train for some journeys. It takes longer, but it's more comfortable and often cheaper. At every stop, local people climb onto the train to sell drinking water, fried snacks or even whole meals wrapped in brown paper or a banana leaf.

Boats and ships

There are as many different kinds of boats in Indonesia as road vehicles. In remote parts of the outer islands, people travel in canoes dug out from whole tree trunks. Modern motor ferries carry passengers and cargo between the islands. Even in Jakarta elegant wooden sailing ships still bring timber from the outer islands, loading up with market goods for the return journey.

People on the move

Eid-ul-Fitr is the biggest holiday in Indonesia. It comes at the end of the Muslim **fasting** month, Ramadan, and the celebrations last for several days. Everyone tries to go home and visit their family for the holiday, and this is the time when all means of transport are full to bursting. The roads are full of private cars, and special buses and trains are arranged so that as many people as possible can be with their families.

Some people will be too far from their village to afford a visit. But in Jakarta especially, many who do will return at the end of the holiday with more members of their family, eager to take their chances in the city.

Looking at Indonesia

A roadside religious shrine on Celebes with gifts of rice, coconuts and flowers.

A man in Jakarta making a large traditional umbrella, probably for a procession.

In this book we have tried to show you that Indonesia includes many different kinds of people and ways of life across the thousands of islands. There are rich people and poor people. There are factory workers, forest hunters, businesspeople and pearl divers, people living in tower blocks and tree houses. They are separated by thousands of kilometres and by different cultures and standards of living.

Unity in diversity

For the newly independent country of Indonesia, the slogan 'Unity in diversity' became very important. This is a way of saying that the strength of the country comes from its many different people, just as a rope has strength from the different strands that make it up.

▷ A boat on the beach at Gilimeno, a small tourist island off Lombok.

▽ A group of children in Padang, Sumatra.

Indonesia is changing rapidly. But most of the economic growth has happened in Java and its cities. Meanwhile people living in the country are often very poor, growing cheap food for city-dwellers.

Much of the wealth for this development has come from the **natural resources** of the outer islands. People here sometimes feel that their own ways of life are being pushed aside by the powerful central government. Islanders feel that they should be given a chance to decide for themselves about their lives and resources, so that 'Unity in diversity' can be a real strength as Indonesia continues to develop.

Glossary

Adat This is Indonesia's unwritten customary village law. It may vary in the different parts of Indonesia, but it does not depend on the religion your family follows.

Archipelago A geographical word which means a group of islands.

Bahasa Indonesia The national language, based on a trader's dialect of Malay. A shared language is very useful, but most people along the archipelago teach their children the local language and customs, too.

Buddhism This religion began in India in 500 BC and spread all over the world. Buddhists teach that by rejecting our greed and desire we will leave the suffering of this life and find heaven (Nirvana).

Cash crop A crop which is grown to be sold rather than eaten by the farmers themselves. Some are food and drink, like rice or coffee, and some are for use by industry, like rubber or timber.

Colony When settlers take over a country, and claim it as their own, or for their own country, they colonize it.

Development This word can be used in different ways. Bankers might use it to describe the growth of industry in a poor country. But it can also describe the way communities build systems of education, health, culture and social justice.

Exports Goods sold and transported to other countries.

Fasting To go without food for a period of time. Often for religious reasons.

Foreign exchange A way of describing 'international money' used for trading imports and exports between countries.

Hinduism One of the oldest religions in the world, dating before 1000 BC. Hinduism has many Gods. Hindus believe in rebirth (reincarnation).

Imports Imports are goods bought from other countries.

Irrigation A way of providing water for crops using specially built channels and pipes.

Islam The religion followed by Muslims. It was founded in the 7th century. Their holy book is called the Qur'an.

Kampung A small village or hamlet. It also describes a neighbourhood, or a living compound in the country or the city.

Manufacturing The way a product is made from raw materials, especially on a large scale using machinery.

Migrate To move from one region, island, or country to another.

Monsoon A wind that changes direction with the seasons. The word is also sometimes used to describe the rainy season in southern Asia.

Muslims People who follow the Islamic religion.

Natural resources The natural products of the Earth. Some are called renewable because if we are sensible, they can be used again and again. Well-farmed land, fish stocks and power from the wind are all renewable. Some are non-renewable and can only ever be used once, like oil, gas and coal.

Self-sufficient When people are able to grow enough food to feed themselves and their families – not relying on other people.

Subsistence farming A type of farming where most or all of what is grown is eaten or used by the farmers and their family, with little or nothing left over to sell.

Transmigration Moving from one part of a country to another under a government scheme.

Transnational companies A company which has business interests in different countries around the world.

Wayang The word means 'shadow' or 'ghost'. It is the name for Javanese theatre that tells a story using real people, solid puppets or the shadows cast by flat leather puppets onto a screen.

Index

About Oxfam in Indonesia

The international family of Oxfams works with poor people and their organizations in over 70 countries. Oxfam believes that all people have basic rights: to earn a living, and to have food, shelter, health care, and education. Oxfam provides relief in emergencies, and gives long-term support to people struggling to build a better life for themselves and their families.

Oxfam UK and Ireland works in Indonesia with local voluntary agencies, promoting community development. Oxfam funds improvements in agriculture through soil conservation, tree planting and irrigation programmes. Oxfam also works with coastal communities, supporting co-operative fishing organizations and the protection of fishing grounds. With disadvantaged children, Oxfam helps provide training in health and safety at work and education. With disabled people the programme helps provide training and skills for livelihoods and independence. All of Oxfam's programme in Indonesia seeks to include and help women, who are often the most disadvantaged of the poor.

The publishers would like to thank the following for their help in preparing this book: Paul Valentin and Geraldine Terry of Oxfam's Asia Desk; staff of the Oxfam office in Indonesia; the people of Jatiwakas; Tracey Hawkins of Oxfam's photo library; Angela Grunsell, an Oxfam Primary Education advisor.

The Oxfam Education Catalogue lists a range of other resources on economically developing countries, including Indonesia, and issues of development. These materials are produced by Oxfam, by other agencies, and by Development Education Centres. For a copy of the catalogue contact Oxfam, 274 Banbury Road, Oxford OX2 7DZ, phone (01865) 311311, or your national Oxfam office.

Photographic acknowledgements
The author and publishers wish to acknowledge, with thanks, the following photographic sources:

Robert Harding Picture Library pp4, 11; Nick Barraclough pp7, 26b, 27, 28, 29; Bruce Coleman Ltd p12; all other photos by Susi Arnott

The publishers have made every effort to trace the copyright holders, but if they have inadvertently overlooked any, they will be pleased to make the necessary arrangement at the first opportunity.

Cover photograph: Portrait of Javanese girl, Jeremy Hartley/Panos Pictures

Note to the reader - In this book there are some words in the text which are printed in **bold** type. This shows that the word is listed in the glossary on page 30. The glossary gives a brief explanation of words which may be new to you.

First published in Great Britain by Heinemann Library, an imprint of Heinemann Publishers (Oxford) Ltd Halley Court, Jordan Hill, Oxford OX2 8EJ

OXFORD LONDON EDINBURGH MADRID ATHENS BOLOGNA PARIS MELBOURNE SYDNEY AUCKLAND SINGAPORE TOKYO IBADAN NAIROBI HARARE GABORONE PORTSMOUTH NH (USA)

© 1996 Heinemann Publishers (Oxford) Ltd.
00 99 98 97 96
10 9 8 7 6 5 4 3 2 1

British Library Cataloguing in Publication Data
Arnott, Susi
   Indonesia. – (Worldfocus Series)
   I. Title II. Series
   959.8

ISBN 0 431 07249 3 (Hardback)
ISBN 0 431 07243 4 (Paperback)

Designed and produced by Visual Image
Cover design by Threefold Design
Printed and bound in Britain by Bath Press Colourbooks, Glasgow

A 5% royalty on all copies of this book sold by Heinemann Publishers (Oxford) Ltd will be donated to Oxfam (United Kingdom and Ireland), a registered charity number 202918.

The Channel 4 Schools series, Geographical Eye Over Asia, complements the geographical issues explored in this book. It features family and economic life in Jakarta, and the impact of the local environment on village life in central Java. For details of transmission times or to order the accompanying teachers' guide, please contact: The Educational Television Company Ltd., PO Box 100, Warwick CV34 6TZ. Telephone 01926 433333.